Earth Keepers

HENRY DAVID THOREAU

A Neighbor to Nature

Earth Keepers

HENRY DAVID THOREAU

A Neighbor to Nature

Catherine Reef
Illustrated by Larry Raymond

Twenty-First Century Books

A Division of Henry Holt and Co., Inc.

Frederick, Maryland

Published by
Twenty-First Century Books
A Division of Henry Holt and Co., Inc.
38 South Market Street
Frederick, Maryland 21701

Text Copyright © 1992
Catherine Reef

Illustrations Copyright © 1992
Twenty-First Century Books

All rights reserved. No part of this book may be reproduced or utilized in any form or by any means, electronic or mechanical, including photocopying, recording, or by any information storage and retrieval system, without written permission from Twenty-First Century Books.

Printed in the United States of America

10 9 8 7 6 5 4 3 2 1

Library of Congress Cataloging in Publication Data

Reef, Catherine
Henry David Thoreau: A Neighbor to Nature
Illustrated by Larry Raymond

(An Earth Keepers Book)
Includes glossary and index.
Summary: Describes the life of the author who came to value the natural world and whose writings have influenced and inspired others concerning nature.
1. Thoreau, Henry David, 1817-1862—Biography—Juvenile literature.
2. Authors, American—19th century—Biography—Juvenile literature.
3. Naturalists—United States—Biography—Juvenile literature.
[1. Thoreau, Henry David, 1817-1862. 2. Authors, American. 3. Naturalists.]
I. Raymond, Larry, ill. II. Title.
III. Series: Earth Keepers
PS3053.R4 1991
818'.309—dc20 [B] 91-19779 CIP AC
ISBN 0-941477-39-8

Contents

Chapter 1
    A Proper Nursery 7

Chapter 2
    An Odd Stick 14

Chapter 3
    Nature's Own Child 21

Chapter 4
    Trainer Thoreau 32

Chapter 5
    Here Is Life 41

Chapter 6
    A Curious Passenger 50

Chapter 7
    Into a Far Country 59

Chapter 8
    Life's Dance 66

Glossary 70

Index 72

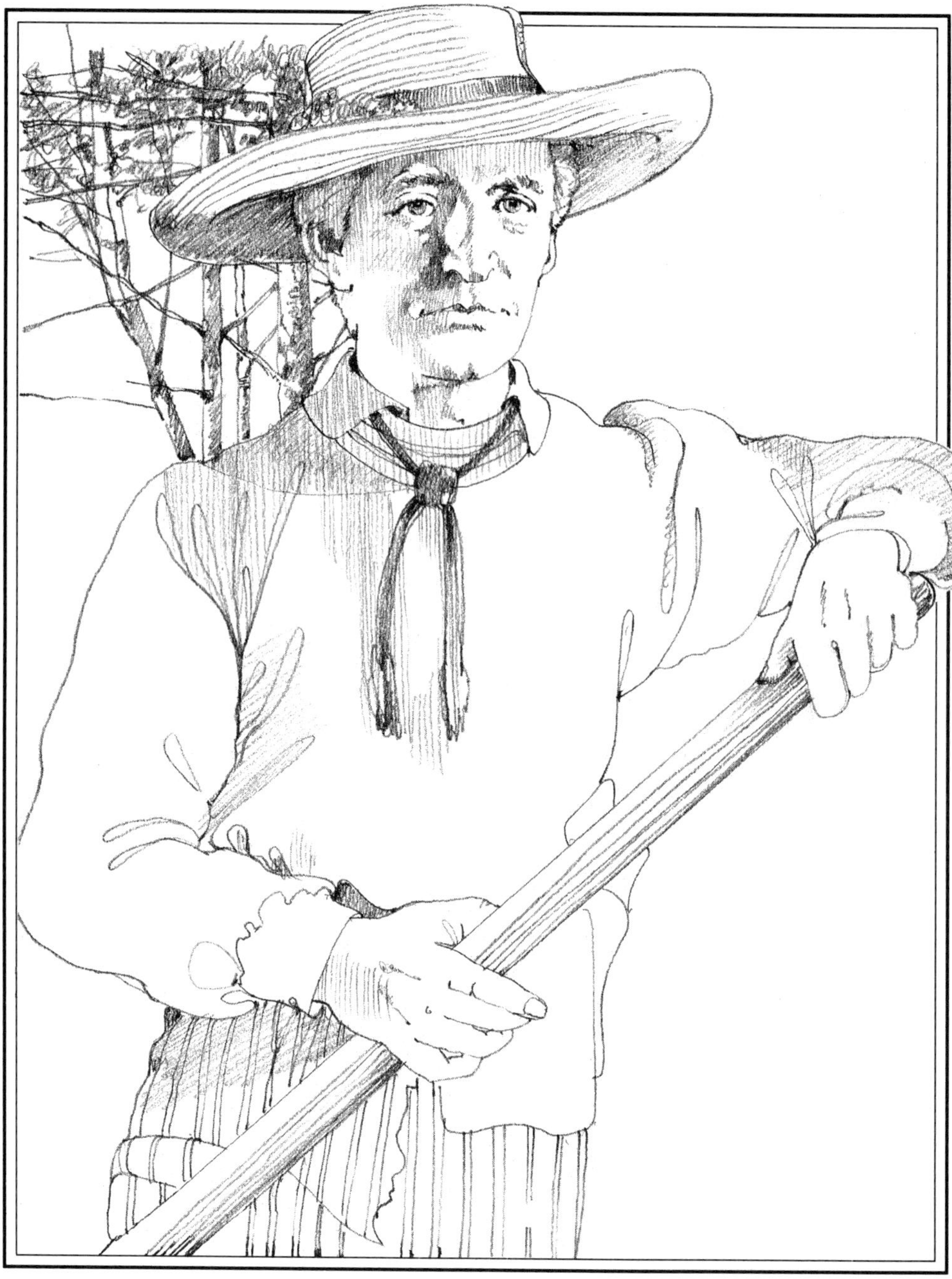

"We can never have enough of Nature."

Chapter 1

A Proper Nursery

Alone, away from his busy, noisy family, a boy looked out of his attic window. He watched martins fly to and from the back-yard birdhouses, building their nests. It was spring, and the shiny, blue-black birds had just returned to Massachusetts from a warm season in South America.

On any other day of the week, young Henry Thoreau could have escaped from his house as freely as the martins flew from theirs. But Henry was not allowed to play on a Sunday.

Sunday, the Sabbath, was a strict day of worship in the 1820s, a day set aside for thinking about God. It was a time when hard-working New Englanders took a break from their weekly labors, a single day of rest before six busy ones of farming, housework, or business. On Sunday, children, too, were supposed to observe the Sabbath and put away their toys and books.

As Henry watched the world from the window that afternoon, a hawk circled overhead. With his sharp, gray eyes, the boy followed the hawk as it flew high over the countryside. For a moment, Henry forgot that he was stuck indoors. His thoughts followed the hawk on its flight. The hawk swooped over the roofs of Concord, Massachusetts, where all of the shops were locked up tightly. Its shadow passed across the farmers' fields and pastures that were carefully boxed in with walls of stone.

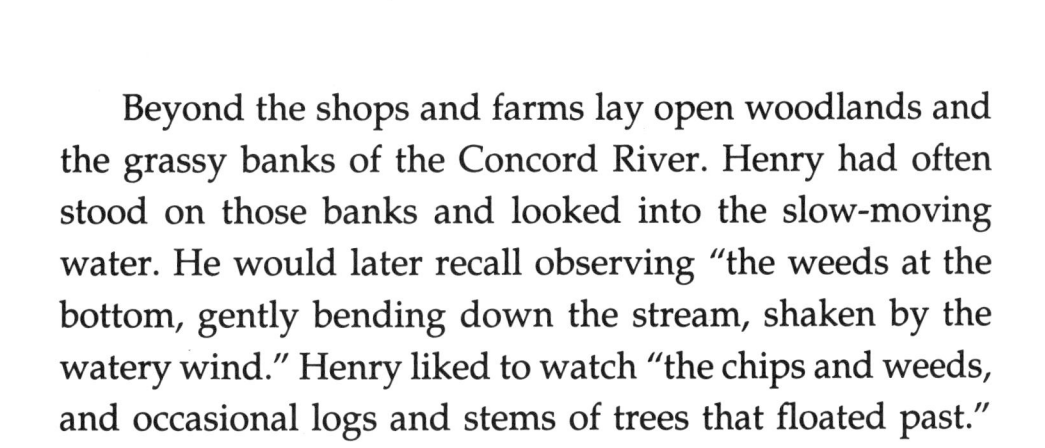

Beyond the shops and farms lay open woodlands and the grassy banks of the Concord River. Henry had often stood on those banks and looked into the slow-moving water. He would later recall observing "the weeds at the bottom, gently bending down the stream, shaken by the watery wind." Henry liked to watch "the chips and weeds, and occasional logs and stems of trees that floated past."

Near the town of Concord were several ponds, formed when a glacier—a huge, moving wall of ice—passed over the area 10,000 years ago. Henry loved the sight of sunlight reflected from the surfaces of these ponds. "Great crystals on the surface of the earth," he called the sparkling bodies of water. Sometimes he imagined that they were "Lakes of Light."

Walden Pond was one of Henry's favorite spots. Even as a very young child, he could stand alone among the trees at Walden Pond and not feel lonely. Instead, he felt peaceful and at one with nature. That feeling, he remembered, was one that "my spirit seemed so early to require." In the pine trees around the pond, his spirit felt "as if it had found its proper nursery."

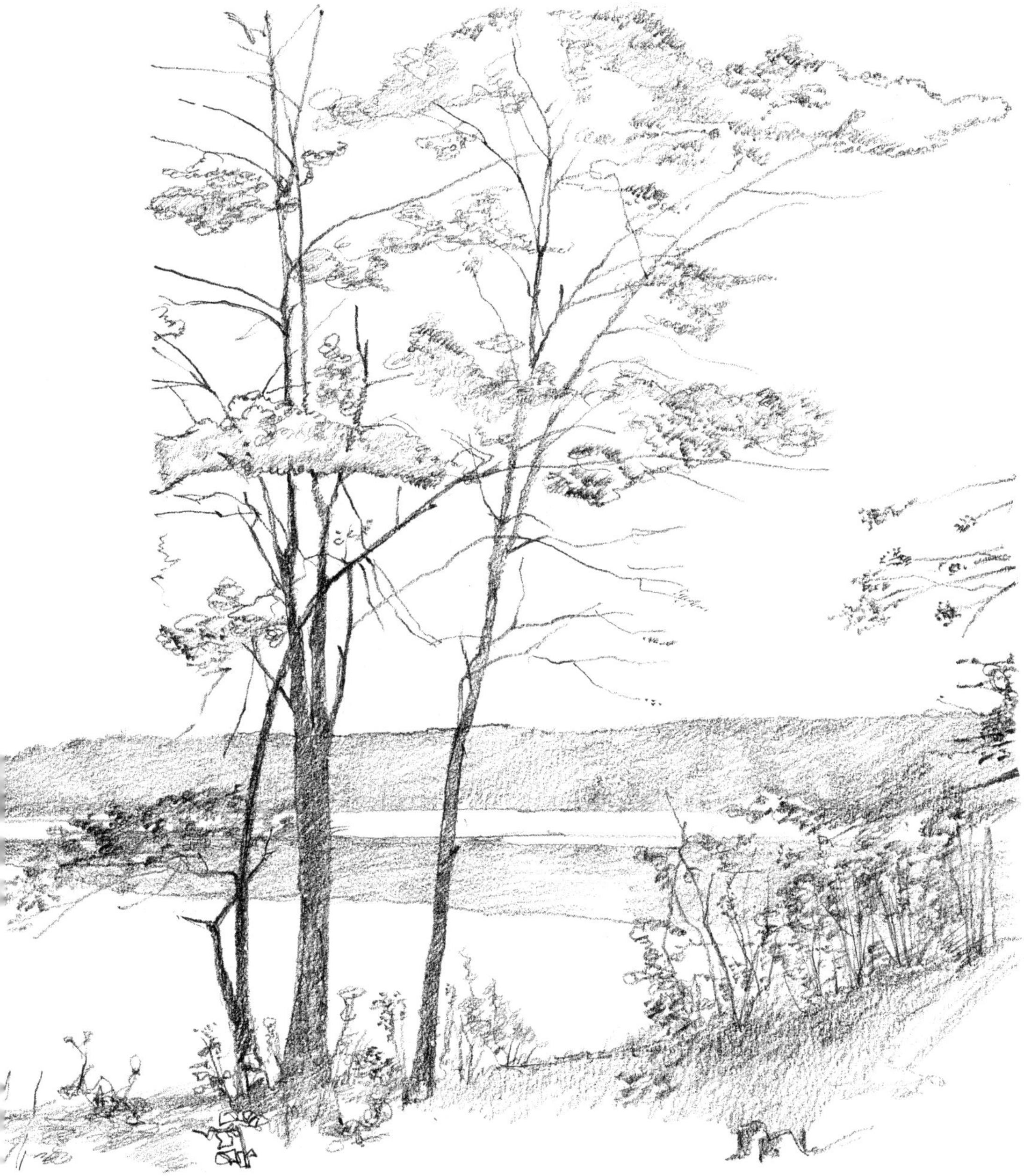

As a grown man, Henry Thoreau returned to Walden Pond. For more than two years—from July 4, 1845, until September 6, 1847—he lived in a one-room cabin that he built on the shore of the pond.

Henry Thoreau went to Walden Pond to live a simple life, a life that was not "frittered away by detail." With his time not taken up with work or other business, he hoped to learn the true meaning of life.

The book he wrote about that experience, *Walden*, has helped many people think about and change their lives. It has shown people that nature is something to be valued and protected. This writer from Concord taught people to value the natural world for more than the lumber, metal, and other goods that it could provide. Nature, Thoreau explained, brought peace of mind and encouraged people to think for themselves.

"We can never have enough of Nature," he wrote. "The wilderness with its living and decaying trees, the thunder clouds, and the rain which lasts three weeks"— Henry Thoreau was at home in natural settings such as these. Away from crowds and the clutter of city life, he thought, people could discover what was lasting, important, and true in the world.

Thoreau saw that people, too, were part of nature and that they needed to live in harmony with wild animals and plants. If people were not careful, he warned, they would destroy resources that could never be replaced. "A river with its waterfalls—meadows, lakes, hills, cliffs or individual rocks, a forest and single ancient trees—such things are beautiful," Thoreau said. "They have a high use which dollars and cents never represent."

Thoreau's words have prompted many people to work to protect the environment, or natural surroundings. They have inspired writers and artists to choose nature as their subject. These people, in turn, have passed on their love of nature to others.

All of these people share a belief that they are saving something precious—something that, once lost, can never be replaced. Many of them gained this understanding by reading the works of Henry David Thoreau.

"How glad I was when I was kept from school."

Chapter 2

An Odd Stick

John and Cynthia Thoreau's third child was born on July 12, 1817. They named him David, after an uncle. But everyone called the boy by his middle name, Henry. In addition to his older sister and brother, Helen and John, Henry had a younger sister, Sophia.

Young Henry grew up in a crowded household that was never quiet or dull. His close-knit family freely talked about the issues of the day. Religion and politics were often the conversation around the dinner table.

Adding to their hectic household, the family took in boarders to earn extra money. Henry enjoyed one boarder, his uncle Charles Dunbar, more than the rest. He delighted in Uncle Charles's odd habits—spending Sundays in the cellar, or falling asleep while shaving. Uncle Charles chose a way of life different from that of most New Englanders. Not willing to work steadily, he drifted in and out of the

Thoreau household. After staying in Concord a few weeks, he would take off without notice to wander along the coast of Maine or to cut hay in Vermont.

It was Cynthia Thoreau's job to keep the house in order. Full of energy, she worked hard, stretching every dollar to provide for her large family. "If she had a crust of bread for dinner," one friend remembered, "she would see that it was properly served."

But although they watched every penny, the Thoreaus often helped others who were less fortunate. At Christmas and Thanksgiving, Cynthia and John invited poor neighbors to share the Thoreau family dinner.

Cynthia's sympathy for other people went beyond her Concord neighborhood. She believed in equality for all people, regardless of race or nationality. Strong-minded and forceful, Cynthia Thoreau spoke out often against the practice of slavery. She founded the Concord Women's Anti-Slavery Society.

John Thoreau, Sr., was a thoughtful man. Honest and friendly, he made wooden pencils, an item that people were just starting to use. When Henry's father was not working, a quiet time reading or playing music would make him happy. He shared his favorite books with Henry and taught him to play the flute.

Both parents enjoyed the outdoors and taught their children to love nature. This was easy to do in Concord, with its nearby trees and waterways. The family hiked to the woods and cooked chowder on a homemade fireplace. Cynthia often called her children outside to listen to the birds sing.

But there was more than nature to learn about in Concord. This town of 2,000 people took pride in its role in American history. The Revolutionary War saw an early battle there. The first gunfire of that battle is famous as "the shot heard 'round the world."

The citizens were proud of their present-day town as well. Concord was the site of a busy county courthouse. Coaches traveling to and from Boston stopped in Concord every day, and travelers often visited the town's shops and hotels. Children loved to watch the barges that moved up and down the Concord River. Sometimes the barge crews even invited them on board.

The education of Concord's children was not left to barge crews, however. At school, children were expected to behave like adults, sitting properly and listening with strict attention to their teachers for long periods.

At the town's public grammar school, students in all grades sat close together on benches. Henry and the others learned to recite long passages from the Bible and William Shakespeare's plays. The teacher punished any boys and girls who did not pay attention by flogging them (hitting them with a stick).

When Henry was 11, he and his brother, John, entered the Concord Academy, a private school. Henry did well in his studies. In one composition, titled "The Seasons," Henry showed his early love of nature. He described the sights and sounds that the changing seasons brought to the natural world.

Henry wrote that in the spring, "the ground begins to look green with the new born grass. The birds which have lately been to more southern countries return again to cheer us with their morning song." Henry called the summer "the pleasantest part of the year," as trees and flowers bloom and fruit begins to swell and ripen.

When autumn comes, "the farmers begin to lay in their Winter's store, and the market abounds with fruit." Birds fly to warmer places, "as they know that Winter is coming." In winter, "there is nothing to be seen," Henry stated. "We have no birds to cheer us with their morning song. We hear only the sound of sleigh bells."

Henry had many chances to witness the changes that occur in nature. He liked nothing better than to spend time alone in the woods and meadows, hunting for Indian arrowheads or skating on the frozen ponds. As an adult, he wrote, "I remember how glad I was when I was kept from school a half a day to pick huckleberries on a neighboring hill all by myself for the family dinner."

As he grew older, Henry found that he liked exploring nature better than playing games with his schoolmates. He did not make friends easily, as his brother, John, did. The other children nicknamed him "Judge" because he seemed so serious. They called him an "odd stick."

Still, Concord's young people could not help admiring Henry's love of the outdoors. They praised him as someone "who did not fear mud or water."

Henry was also known for his ability to work with his hands. He liked to whittle—to carve animals, whistles, and other objects from small pieces of wood. He was so handy with a hammer and nails, in fact, that some of his family thought that he would make a good carpenter.

In the summer of 1833, when he was 16, Henry built a rowboat called "The Rover." In it, he spent peaceful afternoons floating alone on Walden Pond, lying on his back and looking up at the sky. If they had seen him, his busy Concord neighbors might have called Henry lazy.

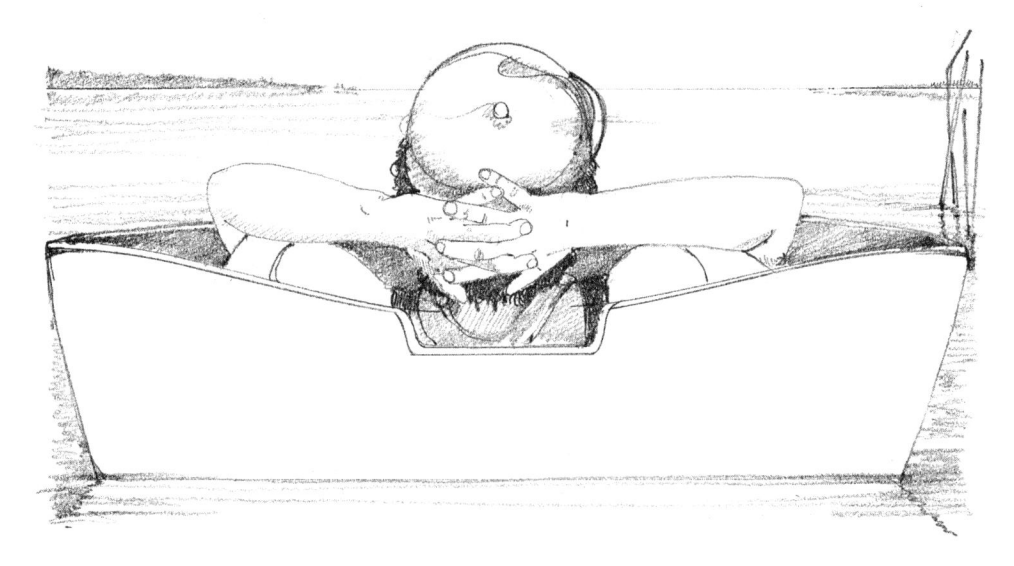

However, Henry, deep in thought, did not believe he was wasting his time. He liked to think of the people—both Native Americans and settlers—who had been at this pond before him and yet had left it clean and unspoiled. For hundreds of years, he thought, people "have drank at it, admired and fathomed it, and passed away, and still its water is green and pelucid [clear] as ever."

"I would make education a pleasant thing."

Chapter 3

Nature's Own Child

Cynthia Thoreau was not about to let Henry become a carpenter. She had other plans for her younger son—she wanted him to go to college. So, on August 30, 1833, Henry traveled 15 miles to Cambridge, Massachusetts, to enter Harvard University.

The 250 students at Harvard worked six busy, tiring days every week. After early morning prayers in the cold college chapel, they spent long days studying Latin, Greek, mathematics, and French.

Henry did not make many friends among the students at Harvard. Some of the other students remarked that he seemed "cold," as if "he did not care for people." Henry clearly felt more at ease by himself, walking along the banks of the Charles River or slipping off to spend time in the nearby fields. One of his college classmates referred to Henry as "Nature's own child."

Henry soon discovered Harvard University's library of 50,000 books. A serious student, Henry read constantly and copied passages that he liked into a notebook.

One of his favorite books was *Nature,* by Ralph Waldo Emerson, one of Concord's own citizens. This short book seemed to express Henry's own feelings about nature.

Nature was the first thing to influence a person's mind, Emerson stated, and the most meaningful. "There is never a beginning, there is never an end," Emerson wrote about nature. He called nature's network of plants and animals "this web of God." Nature, Emerson thought, could lead people to a more spiritual life.

In nature, people could escape from the routines of daily life and see the world with fresh eyes. Away from work, chores, and business cares, Emerson said, people could take time to notice the beauty of the world. They could find wonder in ordinary things—morning sunlight, the laughter of a child, or a summer storm. They could see "the miraculous in the common."

Henry Thoreau almost had to leave Harvard before graduating. In the spring of 1836, he became ill and had to go home for several months. Historians are not certain what illness Henry had, but they think that it might have been tuberculosis. This contagious disease, which usually affects the lungs, was common in the 1800s and caused many deaths.

Some members of Henry's family urged him to leave school. Studying is ruining your health, they warned. But Henry wanted to get back to his studies. Feeling better after a summer's rest in Concord, he returned to Harvard in the fall.

Because he had earned good grades, Henry was invited to give a speech when his class graduated in 1837. His speech made it clear that Henry held ideas that were very different from those of most New Englanders. "This curious world is more beautiful than it is useful," Henry said. "It is more to be admired and enjoyed than used."

Henry did not believe that people should work hard for six days a week and set aside only one day for rest. Instead, Henry suggested, "The order of things should be somewhat reversed; the seventh should be man's day of toil, wherein to earn his living by the sweat of his brow; and the other six his Sabbath."

Henry called upon his fellow students to be "true to their natures" and to lead "independent lives." He spoke against the "love of wealth." Greed and selfishness, Henry feared, were causing people to destroy natural resources. He urged the students not to seek wealth, so that "the earth will be as green as ever, and the air as pure."

After graduation, Henry happily returned to Concord. He would have liked to spend six "Sabbaths" each week enjoying nature. But Henry, too, needed to earn a living. He became a teacher at Concord's Center School, where 90 students crowded together in a single classroom.

Henry had been teaching less than two weeks when a member of the school board came to watch him at work. You must flog the children who don't behave, the board member insisted. This suggestion caused Henry to lose his temper. Upset and angry, he chose six students and, for no reason, flogged them. Then he quit his job.

"I would make education a pleasant thing both to the teacher and scholar," he wrote. "We should seek to be fellow students with the pupil." Henry thought that the best teachers were those who learned from their students.

Most people did not agree with Henry's ideas about education. Henry is a strange one, they said. He must have seemed even odder when he changed his name from David Henry to Henry David. Concord's citizens believed that names were "God given" and not to be changed. Now that David Henry was Henry David, his neighbors were *sure* that he was odd.

When he could not find a teaching job, Henry went to work at his father's pencil factory. At that time, the graphite, or "lead," in American pencils broke easily. Henry decided to improve the pencils his family made.

He went to the Harvard library and read everything he could about pencils. He learned that German pencil makers mixed their graphite with a special clay to keep the lead from breaking. Henry soon found a place to buy the clay. He even invented a machine to grind the lead more finely, which also made the pencils sturdier.

Although the family business grew more profitable following these improvements, working at the pencil factory bored Henry. He traveled to Maine in search of a teaching job, but he could not find a position.

Back in Concord, Henry began to spend time with Emerson, the author of *Nature*. Emerson loaned him books from his library and introduced Henry to Concord's other writers and philosophers. Concord had become the home of several authors and thinkers who regularly gathered at Emerson's house.

Emerson had a chance to learn from Henry on the many walks they took to Walden Pond. Emerson enjoyed walking with Henry. "He knew the country like a fox or a bird," Emerson said. "He knew every track in the snow or on the ground, and what creature had taken this path before him."

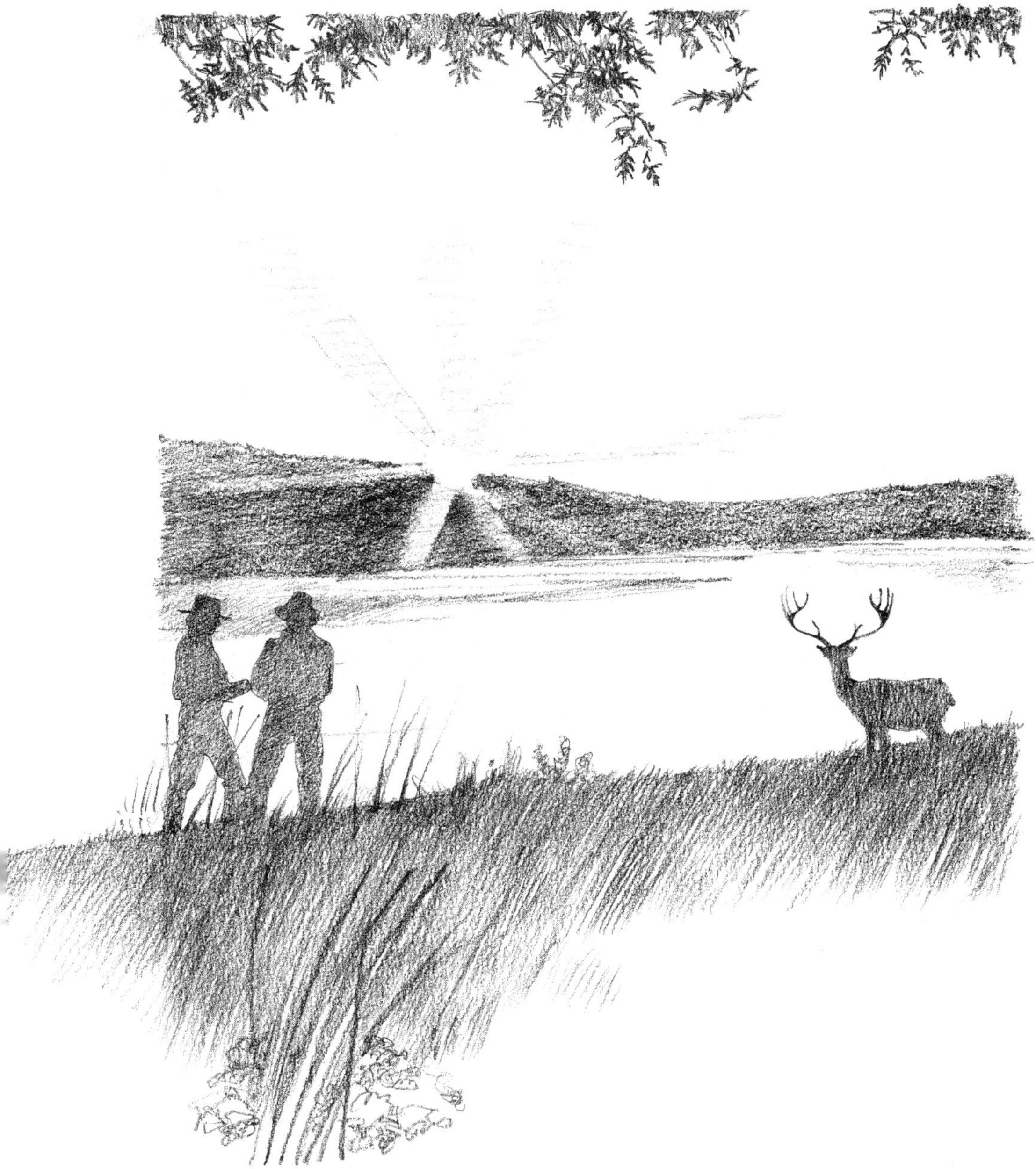

The writers who met at Emerson's home were known as transcendentalists. They believed in a new idea about learning. The transcendentalists thought that when people are born, they already possess a kind of knowledge. There is in each person, they believed, an inborn idea of what is true and good.

According to the transcendentalists, people have an inner voice, or conscience, that reminds them about this knowledge. The transcendentalists said that children often listen to that inner voice. People who live simple, natural lives are able to hear it, too, they believed.

But as people grow up and lead their busy lives, they lose touch with their inner voice. The transcendentalists urged adults to listen to that voice once more. One way for people to do this, they said, is to spend time in nature, away from the many cares and concerns of everyday life.

The transcendentalists liked to keep journals in which they wrote down their ideas. Thinking about what to write helped them listen to their inner voice. Keeping a journal was a way of discovering their true selves, a way of finding out who they really were and what they really wanted to be. Sometimes they used passages from their journals in the books and articles that they wrote.

Henry decided that he, too, would become a writer. He would keep a journal of his own.

On October 22, 1837, when he was 20 years old, Henry David Thoreau opened a blank notebook. There, he wrote the following words: "I make my first entry today."

"Am I not made of Concord dust?"

Chapter 4

Trainer Thoreau

On September 15, 1838, Thoreau placed a notice in the *Yeoman's Gazette*, a local newspaper. It announced that a new school had opened to "a limited number of pupils." The new teacher was "Henry D. Thoreau, Instructor."

Although Thoreau wanted to be a writer, he could not expect to sell books and articles right away. Learning to write well would take time and hard work, and Thoreau needed some way to earn money in the meantime. He decided to open a school of his own. Henry's brother, John, also taught there.

As might be expected, the Thoreaus' school was not like other schools in the 1800s. At most schools, children remained in their seats all day, except for short recesses. But Henry and John took their students on weekly walks to observe animals and flowers. They took them for boat rides on the nearby rivers and for afternoon swims in one of Concord's ponds.

33

The children listened to Henry talk about nature as they walked, sometimes running to catch their teacher by the hand. "If anything happened in the deep woods which only came about once in a hundred years," the children liked to say, "Henry Thoreau would be sure to be on the spot at the time and know the whole story." They called Henry "Trainer Thoreau" because he stood up straight as a soldier. ("Trainer" was a slang word for soldier.)

Henry Thoreau liked to take his pupils to the sites of old Indian villages and camps. Grass had covered most traces of New England's earlier inhabitants. But Thoreau knew how to feel carefully in the earth with a shovel until he found the scorched rocks of an old Indian fireplace. Not wanting to spoil the natural scene, Thoreau would carefully bury the rocks again.

Thoreau's pupils learned why Native Americans had settled at the site. The children looked for springs that provided fresh water and hills that offered shelter from the cold winter winds. They also learned about the Native American way of life. The Indian tribes took from nature only what they needed. The Indians saw themselves as part of the natural world, not as people who had come to conquer or destroy it.

Thoreau's students also learned by seeing how things were really done—and by doing them. They went to the newspaper office to see how the local paper was printed. They visited a gunsmith's shop to learn how guns were made. They practiced surveying, or measuring the land.

Flogging was not allowed at this school. Instead, each child promised to behave and study. "If you come to idle and play, or to see other boys study," the brothers warned, "we shall not want you for a pupil." Punishments were not needed, though. The students enjoyed this relaxed and pleasant way of learning. Their behavior was good, and they did well at their studies.

When summer vacation came, Henry and John built a new rowboat. They called it "Musketaquid," the Indian name for the Concord River. They packed their boat with potatoes and melons, pots and pans. Then, with a shove, Henry and John launched the boat—and themselves—on a new adventure. For two weeks, they traveled on the Concord and Merrimack rivers, far into New Hampshire.

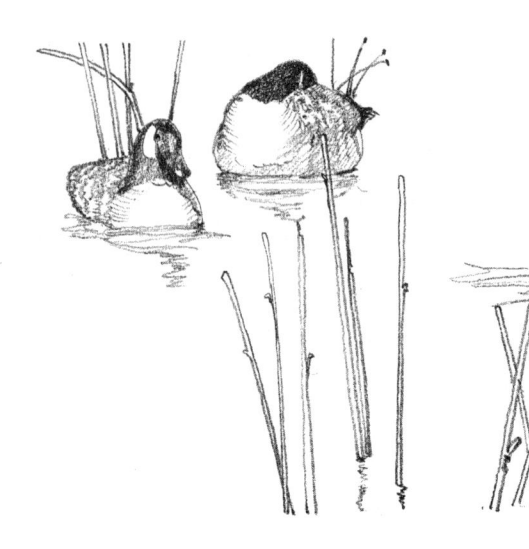

Settlers recently had come to some of the places the brothers passed. Henry saw new towns that seemed to have sprung up in the woods "like the sand-heaps of fresh fox-burrows." He was delighted to see a "border of wild wood"—tall pines and maples—around these towns. "Our lives need the relief of such a background, where the pine flourishes and the jay still screams," he wrote.

Henry and John Thoreau never had another adventure together. In 1840, John became ill. Instead of getting better as the weeks passed, he grew thin and weak. John had tuberculosis and was no longer strong enough to teach. Henry did not want to run their school alone, so he closed the Concord Academy in March of 1841.

Again, Thoreau faced the old problem of how to earn a living. A few of his poems had been published, but he had not yet made any money from his writing.

So Thoreau began to do odd jobs, including some unpleasant chores. Once, he shoveled out a pigpen for 75 cents. In low spirits, Thoreau wrote in his journal, "I will build my lodge on the southern slope of some hill and there take the life the gods send me."

Before he had time to build that lodge, though, Emerson invited Thoreau to live in his large, old house. It seems that Emerson did not share Thoreau's ability as a handyman around the house. A deal was soon made. With his skilled hands, Thoreau would spend a few hours each day doing chores. In return, Henry could use Emerson's library and have time to write.

Thoreau moved into a small bedroom in the Emerson home and quickly proved how handy he was. He planted the garden, cleaned out the chimneys, and even built Mrs.

Emerson a drawer for her gloves. But Thoreau was more than a handyman to the Emersons. When Emerson was away on his lecture tours, he was relieved to know that Thoreau would be there to watch over his family.

Thoreau formed a lasting friendship with the Emerson children—Waldo, Ellen, Edith, and Edward. He enjoyed the children's company, and they quickly grew to love him, too. "He was to us children the best kind of an older brother," Edward Emerson recalled. "He soon became the guide and companion of our early expeditions afield, and, later, the advisor of our first camping trips."

In the evenings, the children would run to Henry, hug his knees, and lead him to the fireplace. There, he told them stories, "sometimes of the strange adventures of his childhood, or more often of squirrels, muskrats, hawks, he had seen that day."

Thoreau left the Emerson home suddenly in January of 1842. His brother was very sick. John had developed tetanus (also called lockjaw), a serious illness that caused many deaths in the 1800s. Earlier that month, John had cut his finger while shaving. The cut did not seem too bad, so he bandaged it with a cloth. But the wound became infected. There was little that could be done to help John. He died in Henry's arms.

Only two weeks later, Thoreau received another blow when five-year-old Waldo Emerson died of scarlet fever. Thoreau became so stricken with grief that he, too, got sick. "I feel as if years have been crowded into the last month," he wrote in his journal.

Thoreau returned to live with the Emersons, but by 1843, he was ready for some kind of change. He traveled to Staten Island, New York, where he taught the young sons of Emerson's brother, William.

But he soon missed his loved ones and the woods of Concord. He realized that whatever he chose to do, he would have to do it in Concord. "I carry Concord ground in my boots and in my hat," he wrote. "Am I not made of Concord dust?"

"To be awake is to be alive."

Chapter 5

Here Is Life

Back in Concord, Thoreau worked again at his father's pencil factory. While his hands busily made pencils all day long, his mind labored, too. He thought of writing a book about his boat trip with John.

A restless Henry Thoreau grew annoyed that he had no time for this or other writing projects. There had to be a better way to live, he thought. It did not make sense for people to spend so much time doing work they did not enjoy. "We live meanly, like ants," Thoreau believed, working for things we don't need—for "more and richer food, larger and more splendid houses, finer and more abundant clothing."

It would be better, Thoreau thought, if people worked only for what was "necessary of life"—simple food and fuel for cooking it, and just enough clothing and shelter to stay warm. If people worked only to meet these needs, they would have the freedom to discover and enjoy life.

Thoreau decided to try an experiment. He would live a life of simplicity—an uncomplicated life, free of luxuries. He would also practice economy, making the best use of his money and resources. That way, he would have time to write, to think, and to learn what was important in life.

The idea of trying this style of living excited Thoreau. "Here is life," he announced, "an experiment to a great extent untried by me." The place for Thoreau's experiment was provided by Emerson, who had recently purchased some property on the shores of Walden Pond. He gave Thoreau permission to live there.

So it was that in the spring of 1845, when he was 27 years old, Thoreau went out to Walden Pond. He chose a spot near the pond to build his cabin and dug a cellar in the sandy soil. Emerson and other neighbors helped Thoreau to raise the roof and put up the walls. The cabin was just the right size to keep one person warm and dry. It was as snug as "an overcoat," observed one of Thoreau's friends.

Thoreau moved into his cabin on July 4, Independence Day, bringing only a few furnishings—his bed, his desk, a table and chairs, and utensils for cooking and eating. "Simplify, simplify," he reminded himself. The simple life was Thoreau's personal declaration of independence.

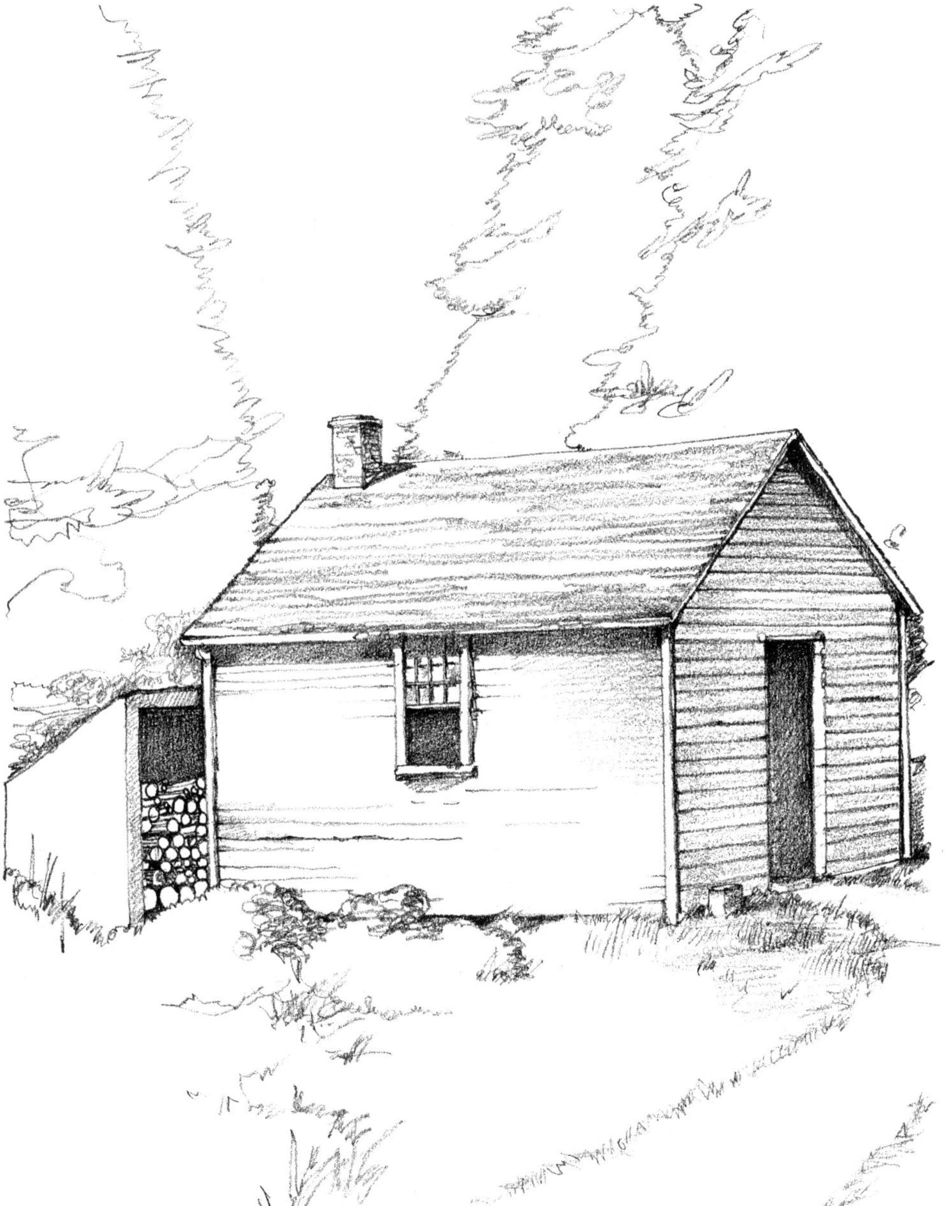

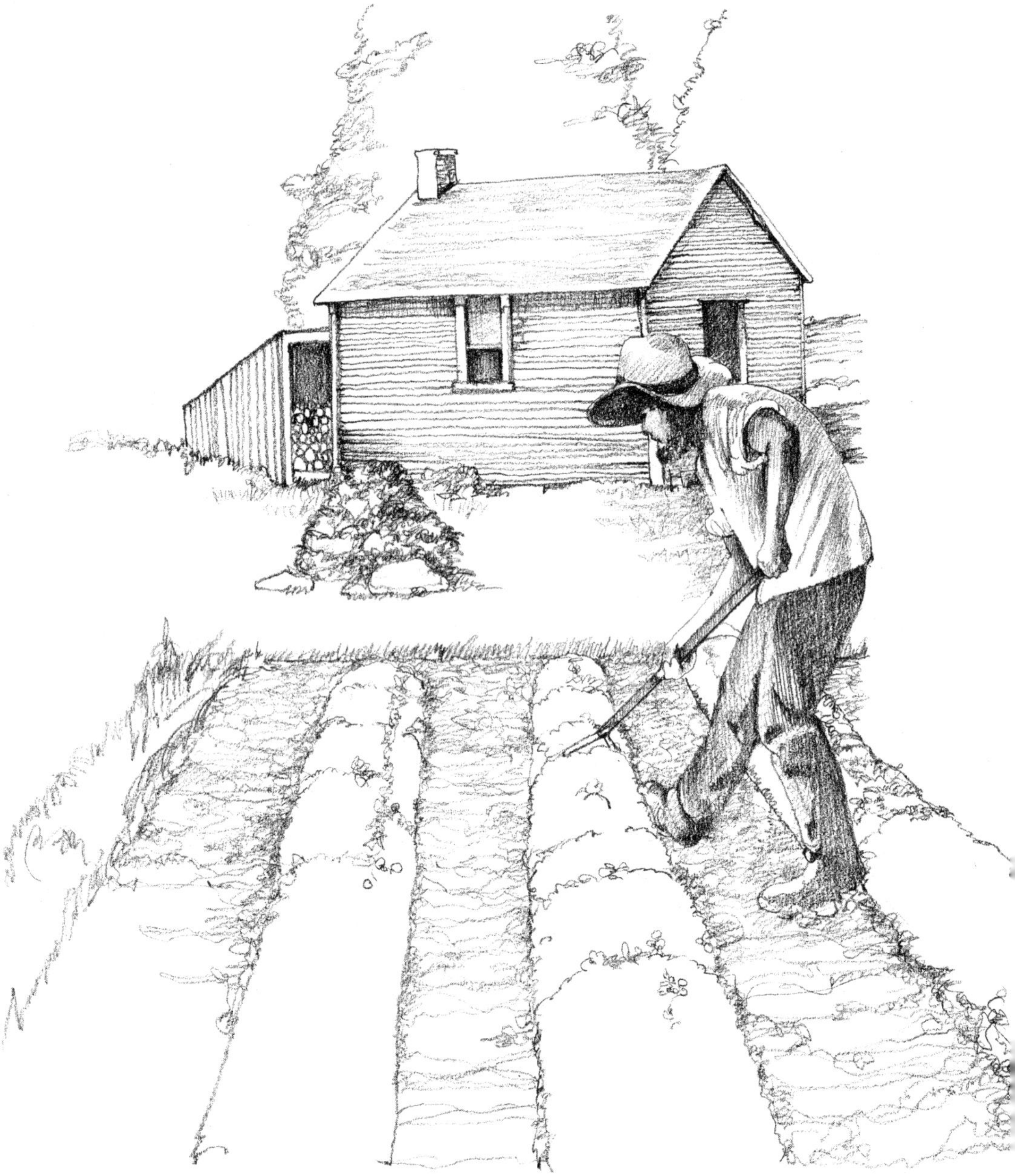

In his new home, Thoreau woke up early each day. He found the morning to be a time when his spirit felt renewed, washed clean of the previous day's concerns. It was also the time when he was most awake and open to new ideas. Morning was "the awakening hour," Thoreau wrote, a time when "there is a dawn in me."

Few people ever feel truly awake, Thoreau believed. They miss opportunities every day to think and learn. "To be awake is to be alive," Thoreau said.

As the morning passed, Thoreau did his daily chores. He swept out his cabin and, on pleasant days, tended to his small garden. "I came to love my rows, my beans," Thoreau wrote. "They attached me to the earth, and so I got strength."

In colder weather, Thoreau worked at odd jobs for a dollar a day. He put up fences and painted buildings. He built a fireplace for one man and a woodshed for another. In this way, Thoreau earned enough money in just six weeks to support himself for a year. "To maintain one's self on this earth is not a hardship but a pastime, if we will live simply and wisely," Thoreau observed.

But some days were too beautiful for working. "There were times when I could not sacrifice the bloom of the present moment to any work," Thoreau recalled.

When birds sang and the sun shone, he liked to sit for hours in his doorway. Pine, hickory, and sumac trees stretched their branches overhead. Sand cherries—pretty to look at but too sour to eat—lined the path that led to Walden Pond. Thoreau would not make a sound. He did not want to disturb the birds that chirped in the trees and flew through his cabin's open windows.

Thoreau also enjoyed rowing on the pond and looking down through the clear water at the fish below—the perch and shiners. "On warm evenings I frequently sat in the boat playing the flute," he wrote, "and saw the perch, which I seemed to have charmed, hovering around me, and the moon travelling over the ribbed bottom, which was strewed with the wrecks of the forest."

Thoreau lived alone at Walden Pond, but he was not lonely. He often visited with his family. He had dinner with the Emersons, and they joined him for picnics and blueberry picking in the woods.

Others came to see him, too. "I had more visitors when I lived in the woods than at any other period in my life," he wrote. When Concord's citizens wanted a break from life in town, they often took walks to Walden Pond. Many came to Thoreau's door, eager to talk with him. They were curious about how he lived in the woods. Thoreau called these visitors "honest pilgrims, who came to the woods for freedom's sake."

One of Thoreau's favorite visitors was a bushy-haired woodcutter by the name of Alek Therien. "A more simple and natural man it would be hard to find," Thoreau wrote. Therien, with his muscular, sunburned neck, was so full of "animal spirits," Thoreau observed, "that he sometimes tumbled down and rolled on the ground with laughter at anything which made him think and tickled him."

Concord's children also visited Thoreau. With them he was an eager teacher, as ever. "He could lead one to the ripest berries, the hidden nest, the rarest flowers," one girl remembered. The children learned from Thoreau not just to love nature but to protect and preserve it. "No plant life could be destroyed," the girl added, "no mother bird could lose her eggs."

Sometimes, escaped slaves came to Thoreau's cabin as they traveled to Canada on the Underground Railroad. The Underground Railroad was a secret network of people who helped escaped slaves reach freedom in the North. Like other members of his family, Thoreau wanted to end the practice of slavery. He would provide a night's shelter to these frightened people, who "listened from time to time, like the fox in the fable, as if they heard the hounds a-baying on their track."

Thoreau came to Walden Pond not just to live a simple life. He also wanted to write. In a year he completed a book about his boat trip with John called *A Week on the Concord and Merrimack Rivers*. He also started another book about his life in the woods.

This book told curious readers how he lived and why he wasn't lonely or afraid. It explained what Thoreau had learned from his experiment and encouraged people to pursue their own dreams. It urged them to try their own experiments in living.

It was a book called *Walden*.

"Be a Columbus to whole new continents."

Chapter 6

A Curious Passenger

Walden gave a complete account of Henry Thoreau's life at the pond. There, Thoreau lived so close to nature that he learned many of its secrets. He watched the cycles of birth and death. More carefully than ever before, he observed the changes that occurred with each season.

Thoreau noticed how the woodland animals depended on one another for food. When the frogs' eggs hatched, for example, the pond was filled with tadpoles. The large number of offspring enabled the species to survive. But the tasty tadpoles also provided food for other animals. There were plenty of tadpoles for the herons and other birds to "gobble up."

It didn't please Thoreau to see animals die. Sometimes it seemed to him that the woods "rained flesh and blood." But in this way, he realized, no one kind of animal grew too plentiful and upset the natural balance. The cycle of birth and death was part of nature's order.

It interested Thoreau to observe how animals' physical traits helped them to survive. One winter evening, a hare sat near his door, keeping perfectly still. To Thoreau, it looked like "a poor wee thing, lean and bony, with ragged ear and sharp nose."

However, as he stepped toward the hare, "away it scud with an elastic spring over the snow crust." Thoreau saw that the hare's thin body was not a sign of ill health. It allowed the animal to escape quickly from danger. "Not without reason was its slenderness," he wrote.

Thoreau also marveled at nature's beauty, which could show up in surprising ways—even in the color of a fish. He noticed that the pickerel (spotted fish that lived in Walden Pond) possessed "a rare beauty." Like the water surrounding them, their colors seemed to change. "They are not green like pine, nor gray like stones, nor blue like the sky," Thoreau noted. Instead, the pickerel had "yet rarer colors, like flowers and precious stones, as if they were pearls."

Thoreau learned he could never be lonely in nature. Like the Native American people who had once lived in Concord's woods, he saw that human beings were a part of nature, not separate from it. "I found myself suddenly neighbor to the birds," he wrote.

Walden Pond was Thoreau's most constant neighbor, and he watched it change with the seasons.

Walden Pond was so deep that its water remained cool even under the hot summer sun. On still summer days, the smooth surface of the pond reminded Thoreau of glass.

In November, the water often appeared dimpled, as if rain had started to fall. But this happened even when the weather was dry. The dimples were caused by small, bronze-colored fish called perch "sporting" in the water.

In winter, Thoreau would lie down on the frozen pond and look at the bubbles trapped deep within the ice. The bubbles were "very clear and beautiful," he wrote. "You see your face reflected in them through the ice."

In spring, new buds on the trees around the pond gave "a brightness to the landscape, especially on cloudy days, as if the sun were breaking through mists and shining faintly on the hill-sides here and there."

Thoreau liked to think of Walden Pond as "the earth's eye." He imagined the trees along the shore to be "the slender eyelashes which fringe it, and the wooded hills and cliffs around it are its overhanging brows." Thoreau often saw himself reflected in this eye, just as a person who looks closely into a real eye sees his or her reflection there. And as Thoreau looked at himself, he saw how he had changed.

When he was younger, Thoreau thought that Walden Pond would always remain a natural and unspoiled place. "When I first paddled a boat on Walden," he recalled, "it was completely surrounded by thick and lofty pine and oak woods."

But now Thoreau knew that humans could destroy the natural world. Because people wanted products made from wood, the trees near Walden Pond were being cut down. "The woodchoppers have still further laid them to waste," Thoreau wrote, "and now for many a year there will be no more rambling through the aisles of wood."

The lumber cutting did more than spoil the view. It hurt wildlife as well. "How can you expect the birds to sing," Thoreau asked, "when their groves are cut down?"

People were changing this natural place in other ways, too. New railroad tracks ran near the pond's border. The train whistles sounded to Thoreau "like the scream of a hawk sailing over some farmer's yard." The citizens of Concord talked about piping water from Walden Pond into their town.

Thoreau thought about people's views toward nature. Many looked upon the wilderness as a strange and even frightening place. Others valued nature only for its lumber and other raw materials. Yet Henry Thoreau understood that nature has a higher value.

His stay at Walden had taught Thoreau an important lesson about life: new experiences change people, helping them to learn and grow. Through this process, they come to feel fully awake, truly alive.

People could always change their habits, Thoreau said, no matter how settled their lives seemed to be. It was wrong to think that if we have "stone-walls piled up on our farms, bounds are henceforth set to our lives and our fates decided."

Thoreau asked his readers to experiment with their lives. He challenged them not simply to accept what life brought their way, but to travel through life like "curious passengers" looking out from their ship. "Be a Columbus to whole new continents and worlds within you, opening up new channels, not of trade, but of thought," he advised.

Thoreau had changed his life when he moved to the pond. As he parted branches to walk through the trees, he came upon exciting new sights and sounds, new ideas and feelings. But soon his Walden home grew familiar. He noticed that his feet "wore a path from my door to the pond-side."

But it was not this footpath that disturbed Thoreau. It was "the paths which the mind travels" that he worried about. Thoreau realized that he was growing used to his surroundings and his routine. He had fewer new ideas. It surprised him to learn how quickly and easily people "fall into a particular route and make a beaten track for ourselves."

By the summer of 1847, Henry Thoreau knew that if he wished to keep learning and growing—to remain fully awake and alive—he would have to make another change. Thoreau saw that it was now time to leave the pond.

"I left the woods for as good a reason as I went there," he wrote in *Walden*. "Perhaps it seemed to me that I had several more lives to live, and could not spare any more time for that one."

Thoreau left Walden Pond on September 6, 1847—two years, two months, and two days after he moved there. Now 30 years old, he was ready for new experiments.

But he would never forget the lesson of Walden Pond. He shared that lesson with his readers:

"I learned this, at least, by my experiment, that if one advances confidently in the direction of his dreams, and endeavors to live the life he has imagined, he will meet with a success unexpected in common hours."

"Death is as near to you as it is to me."

Chapter 7

Into a Far Country

One July evening in 1846, while he was still living at Walden Pond, Thoreau walked to the village of Concord. He wanted to pick up a shoe that had been repaired and to visit with his Concord neighbors. Thoreau called the village a "great news room." It was a place, he said, where gossip passed "from mouth to mouth, or from newspaper to newspaper." Once in a while, Thoreau enjoyed some gossip. He found it to be "as refreshing in its way as the rustle of leaves and the peeping of frogs."

On that July evening, Thoreau ran into Constable Sam Staples, Concord's police officer. But Staples didn't want to stand and gossip. Instead, he expressed concern that Thoreau had not paid his poll tax for six years. Every man between the ages of 20 and 70 was required to pay this tax. If Thoreau did not soon pay the taxes that he owed, Staples warned, he would be locked up in jail.

Thoreau had not paid his poll tax on purpose. He did not want to support a government that allowed slavery. Also, the United States at that time was fighting a war with Mexico. Thoreau believed that the United States was trying to acquire new territory for southern slave owners. He objected strongly to the war and refused to support it with his tax money.

Thoreau decided to follow his conscience rather than obey the law. Before he would pay his poll tax, he stated, the United States "must cease to hold slaves and to make war on Mexico." As for going to jail, Thoreau said, he might go "as well now as any time, Sam."

So the constable arrested Thoreau and took him to Concord's jail, a building with a thick door of wood and metal and even thicker walls of stone. Thoreau, who tried to live life to the fullest, wanted to learn everything he could about life in jail. To Thoreau, spending a night in jail "was like travelling into a far country, such as I never expected to behold."

Through the jail's barred window, he listened to the sounds of Concord's streets at night. He spoke with his cell mate, who had been arrested for setting a barn on fire. The fellow seemed so pleasant that Thoreau decided he had probably fallen asleep while smoking.

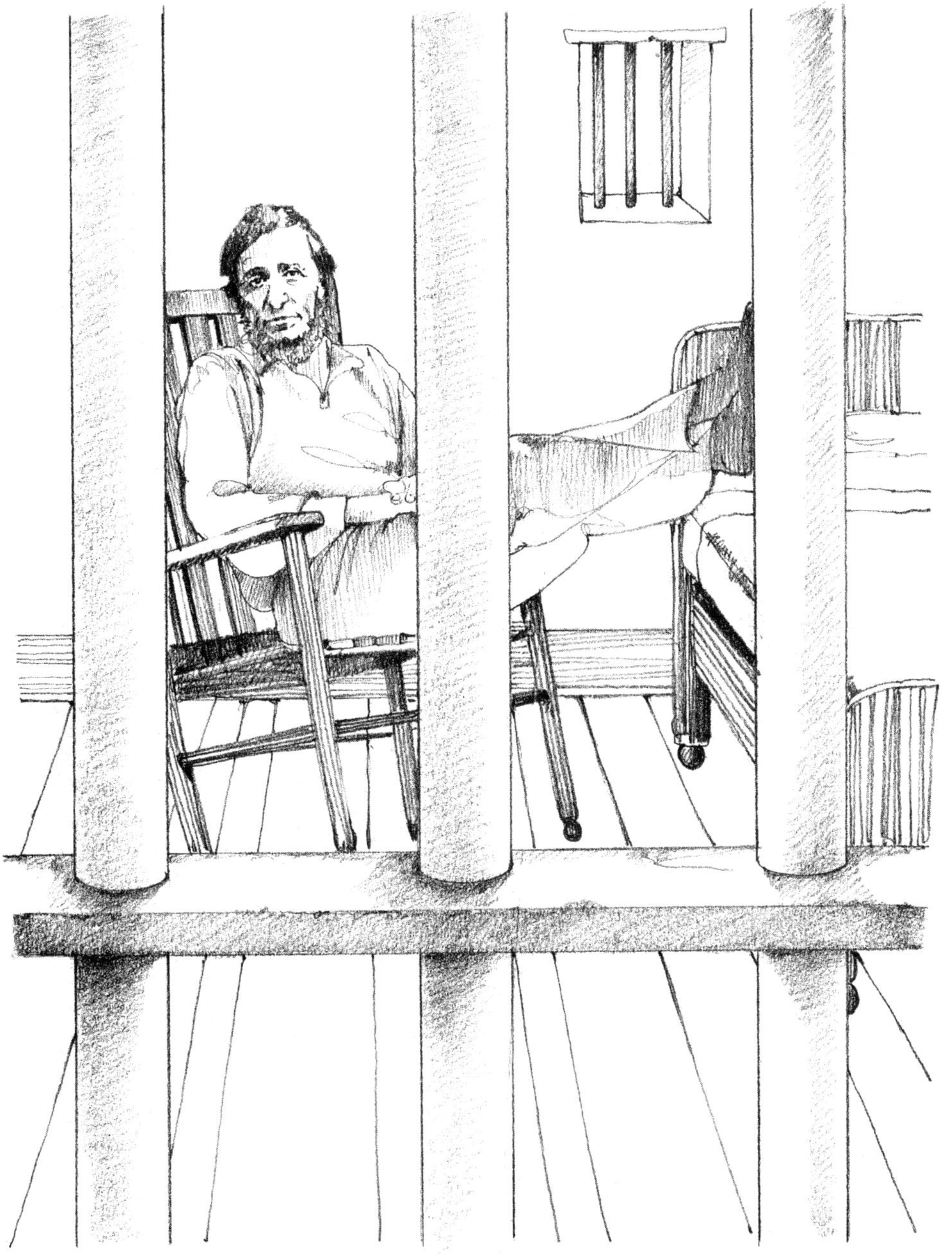

The news of Henry's arrest soon reached the Thoreau family. During the night, someone—it may have been one of Thoreau's relatives—came to the constable's office and paid his taxes.

Staples was ready to release Thoreau in the morning, but there was one problem: Thoreau did not want to leave. He wanted people to learn about his jailing. He hoped it would draw their attention to the issue of slavery. But Sam Staples told him, "Henry, if you will not go of your own accord, I shall put you out, for you cannot stay here any longer."

So Thoreau left the jail and joined some friends to pick berries. Later, he wrote an essay about his night in jail. Known today as "On the Duty of Civil Disobedience," this essay urges people to listen to the inner voice of their own conscience instead of unjust laws. If enough people followed this advice, Thoreau believed, they could peacefully bring about needed changes.

In 1857, Thoreau again acted to oppose slavery. John Brown, a fiery antislavery leader, came to Concord to raise money for his cause. Brown was in favor of using force to free the slaves, but he never explained exactly how this would be done. Although Thoreau did not have much money, he gave some to help Brown's cause.

Thoreau was living in his family's home in October of 1859, working as a handyman and a surveyor, when he learned how John Brown planned to end slavery. News reached Concord that Brown and his followers had raided the government armory, a place for storing weapons, in Harpers Ferry, Virginia (today a part of West Virginia). They hoped that their attack would give the area's slaves enough courage to revolt. They also wanted to form a new state, one that did not allow slavery.

Their plans did not succeed. U.S. government troops defeated Brown's men, killing or capturing most of them. Brown himself had been wounded and was in jail under heavy guard.

John Brown was hanged on December 2, 1859. Thoreau later wrote that even though the government had killed Brown, it had not killed his cause. Brown "is more alive than he ever was," Thoreau said, because he lived on in people's minds and hearts. "He is no longer working in secret. He works in public, and in the clearest light that shines on the land."

By 1860, disagreement about slavery was moving the nation toward the Civil War. But Henry Thoreau, once so outspoken about slavery, now paid little attention to the news of war. He had grown weak from tuberculosis.

As he had done throughout his life, he turned again to nature, with its power to heal and give strength.

He began taking nighttime walks to experience the sights and sounds of nature after dark. At night, even the town of Concord, a place he knew so well, seemed like an exciting, unexplored land. "I frequently had to look up at the opening between the trees above the path in order to learn my route," he said, "and, where there was no cart-path, to feel with my feet the faint tracks which I had worn."

In the spring of 1860, Thoreau took a trip to Minnesota, hoping to find drier air that might help to heal his lungs. But he returned to Concord sicker than when he left. "I have been sick so long," he wrote, "that I have almost forgotten what it is to be well."

Thoreau spent the last few months of his life in the parlor of his family's home, too weak to go upstairs. His friends often came to see him. Even Constable Sam Staples paid a call. Staples told Emerson that he "never saw a man dying with so much pleasure and peace."

Thoreau did not face death with fear. "When I was a boy, I learned that I must die, so I am not disappointed now," he told one friend. "Death is as near to you as it is to me."

His friends' visits pleased Thoreau, but he wished the neighborhood children would come to see him more often. "I love them as if they were my own," he confessed.

Thoreau woke up sicker than ever on the morning of May 6, 1862. He managed to whisper the words "moose" and "Indian," as if he imagined himself back in the Maine woods. Then he closed his eyes and died.

He was buried in a small cemetery in Concord under a simple tombstone that bore a single word: Henry.

"Let us keep the New World new."

Chapter 8

Life's Dance

Henry David Thoreau did not die a famous author. *A Week on the Concord and Merrimack Rivers* had sold only a handful of copies. At most, a couple of thousand people had read *Walden*. Few people understood the importance of Thoreau's writings during his lifetime.

One person who did understand was Ralph Waldo Emerson. At Thoreau's funeral, Emerson predicted that Henry Thoreau's fame would grow. "The country knows not yet, or in the least part, how great a son it has lost," Emerson said.

Emerson's prediction was correct. Shortly after Henry Thoreau's death, the *Atlantic Monthly*, a popular magazine, printed some of his essays. *Walden* soon became a well-known book and was reprinted many times. *A Week on the Concord and Merrimack Rivers* was reprinted as well. Thoreau's journal was published in 1906. It filled 14 large volumes and contained more than 2 million words.

Thoreau's essay "On the Duty of Civil Disobedience" has inspired modern leaders to work for peaceful change. One person who read this essay was Mahatma Gandhi, the man who led India to independence from England. "There is no doubt that Thoreau's ideas greatly influenced my movement in India," Gandhi said.

The Reverend Martin Luther King, Jr., also read the essay. He used nonviolent actions such as boycotts, sit-ins, and marches to protest racial prejudice and discrimination against African Americans.

But the work by Thoreau that has affected more people than any other is *Walden*. It has taught the world that nature—unspoiled and unchanged—is to be enjoyed and cherished.

One early reader compared *Walden* to an actual pond, labeling it "cool and refreshing." Another said that "playful humor and sparkling thought appear on almost every page." Decades later, E. B. White, the author of *Charlotte's Web*, called *Walden* "an invitation to life's dance."

Thoreau's writings have encouraged many people to try to protect wilderness and wildlife. As Supreme Court Justice William O. Douglas said, "Thoreau lived when men were appraising trees in terms of board feet, not in terms of watershed protection and birds and music. His protests against that narrow outlook were among the first heard on the continent."

John Muir, who worked to establish national parks and forests, was one of many environmentalists who read Thoreau's writings. The famous biologist Rachel Carson, who warned the world about the dangers of using harmful pesticides, kept Thoreau's journal at her bedside.

The ideas of Henry Thoreau were the seeds for today's environmental movement. As a result of this movement, the United States now contains millions of acres of land—national parks and forests, wildlife refuges, and wilderness areas—all protected from development and misuse. Throughout the world, people are trying to save wildlife habitats before animal and plant species become extinct. People are also working to stop pollution and preserve natural settings in their own communities.

Shortly before he died, Thoreau wrote, "Each town should have a park, or rather a primitive forest, of five hundred or a thousand acres, where a stick should never be cut for fuel." This natural place would be "a common possession forever, for instruction and recreation." Henry Thoreau urged all Americans to work toward this goal.

"Let us keep the New World *new*," he said. Thoreau wanted people to "preserve all the advantages of living in the country."

Near the end of *Walden*, Thoreau wrote, "If a man does not keep pace with his companions, perhaps it is because he hears a different drummer." In other words, a person who listens to his or her inner voice, who follows that "different drummer," might choose a life unlike that of most people. That person might decide to travel, as Thoreau's Uncle Charles did, or to try living in the woods.

Thoreau's inner voice told him to live a simple life close to nature. It encouraged him to follow his conscience in telling right from wrong. And it inspired him to write down his observations and ideas. In the years that have followed, Thoreau's words have helped to make the earth a more peaceful and beautiful place.

Glossary

civil disobedience	the idea that people should refuse to obey unjust laws
economy	as expressed by Thoreau, the idea that people should work only to fulfill the necessities of life
environment	the physical world that surrounds a plant or animal
environmentalist	a person who seeks to protect the natural environment
extinct	no longer in existence; describes a species of plant or animal that has died out
habitat	the physical surroundings where a living thing makes its home
inner voice	a term used by transcendentalists to describe the inborn knowledge of truth and goodness
lockjaw	another name for tetanus
natural resource	a material or product supplied by nature, such as water, air, minerals, or trees
pesticide	a substance, often a strong and poisonous chemical, used to kill insect pests
pollution	the process by which a natural environment is made unclean and unfit for living things

raw material	material taken from nature and used to make products or to produce energy
scarlet fever	a serious, often fatal, infectious disease that occurs most commonly among children
species	a group of similar plants or animals that can produce offspring
survey	to measure the shape of the land and mark off property boundaries
tetanus	a serious infectious illness that enters the body through a wound or cut
transcendentalism	the belief that people have an inborn knowledge of truth and goodness
transcendentalist	a person who accepts the beliefs of transcendentalism
tuberculosis	an infectious disease that commonly affects the lungs
Underground Railroad	a secret organization of people who helped escaped slaves reach freedom
wilderness area	an area of land or water permanently protected from development
wildlife	animals or plants living in a natural state
wildlife refuge	an area of land or water set aside as a protected home for wildlife

Index

Atlantic Monthly 66

Bible 18
Brown, John 62-63

Carson, Rachel 68
Civil War 63
Concord 8, 10, 12, 15-20, 23-26, 28, 32, 40-41, 48, 52, 56, 59-60, 62-65
conscience 30

Douglas, William O. 67
Dunbar, Charles 14-15, 69
"On the Duty of Civil Disobedience" 62, 67

economy 42, 46
Emerson, Ralph Waldo 23, 28-30, 38-40, 42, 48, 64, 66

Gandhi, Mahatma 67

Harpers Ferry 63
Harvard University 21-24, 26

King, Jr., Rev. Martin Luther 67

lockjaw 39

Muir, John 68
"Musketaquid" 36

Native Americans 19-20, 34, 36, 52, 65
natural resources 12-13, 24, 55-56
Nature 23, 28

poll tax 59-60
pollution 68

raw materials 56
Revolutionary War 16-17
"The Rover" 20

scarlet fever 40
"The Seasons" 18
Shakespeare, William 18
slavery 15, 49, 60, 62-63
Staples, Constable Sam 59-60, 62, 64
surveying 35, 63

tetanus 39
Therien, Alek 48
Thoreau, Cynthia 14-16, 21
Thoreau, Helen 14
Thoreau, Jr., John 14, 18-19, 32, 36-39, 41, 49
Thoreau, Sr., John 14-15
Thoreau, Sophia 14
transcendentalism 30
tuberculosis 23, 38, 63-64

Underground Railroad 49

Walden 12, 49-50, 57, 66-69
Walden Pond 10-12, 20, 28, 42-49, 50, 52-59
A Week on the Concord and Merrimack Rivers 49, 66
White, E.B. 67
wilderness area 12, 55, 68
wildlife habitat 68
wildlife refuge 68

Yeoman's Gazette 32